WHAT DOES NEW AMERICA NEED?

Topics of the Constitutional Convention

American Constit...
Children's Govern...

UNIVERSAL POLITICS
✦ POLITICS & SOCIAL SCIENCES ✦

First Edition, 2020

Published in the United States by Speedy Publishing LLC, 40 E Main Street, Newark, Delaware 19711 USA.

© 2020 Universal Politics Books, an imprint of Speedy Publishing LLC

Universal Politics Books are available at special discounts when purchased in bulk for industrial and sales-promotional use. For details contact our Special Sales Team at Speedy Publishing LLC, 40 E Main Street, Newark, Delaware 19711 USA. Telephone (888) 248-4521 Fax: (210) 519-4043.

10 9 8 7 6 * 5 4 3 2 1

Print Edition: 9781541977747
Digital Edition: 9781541977884
Hardcover Edition: 9781541979918

See the world in pictures. Build your knowledge in style.
www.speedypublishing.com

TABLE OF CONTENTS

When you play a board game, you and your opponents, the people with whom you play, are under the same rules. After all, how can you even know who wins or loses, or how to plan strategy, if all players do as they like? It is much the same in government, but the outcomes affect many people.

ALL THE PLAYERS IN A BOARD GAME
MUST FOLLOW THE SAME SET OF RULES.

LAWS NEED TO BE FAIR, AND IF SOMEONE BREAKS THE LAW, THERE NEEDS TO BE CONSEQUENCES.

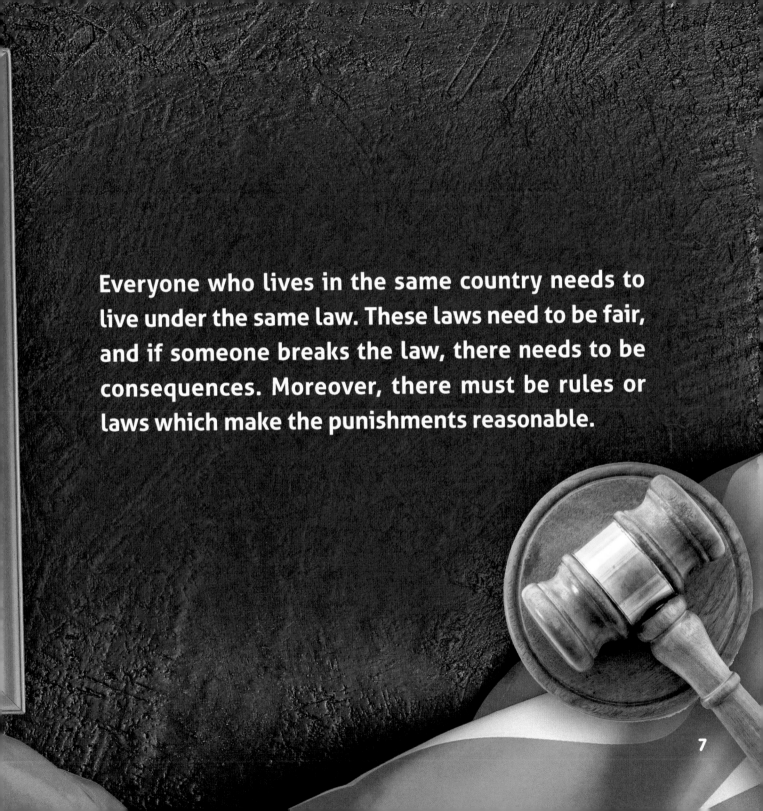

Everyone who lives in the same country needs to live under the same law. These laws need to be fair, and if someone breaks the law, there needs to be consequences. Moreover, there must be rules or laws which make the punishments reasonable.

As a result, countries need a constitution. A constitution lays out the rules about how the government works, how to make new laws, and what principles the laws cannot violate. This book will discuss how the American constitution came to be written and some compromises that had to be made for all the states to agree to its terms.

THE ARTICLES OF CONFEDERATION FAIL

The United States began when thirteen British colonies in North America grew angry at their mistreatment by the British. The King of England was unwilling to compromise with the colonists, and tensions escalated into the American Revolutionary War.

Original 13 British Colonies

New Hampshire

New York

Massachusetts

Rhode Island

Connecticut

Pennsylvania

New Jersey

Delaware

Virginia

Maryland

North Carolina

South Carolina

Georgia

MAP OF THE ORIGINAL 13 BRITISH COLONIES

To all to whom

When the new Americans finally won the war, they had to come up with a new set of rules and government. These new rules were contained in the Articles of Confederation.

Since the colonists, now Americans, had suffered under a powerful government, they were afraid of their freedoms being taken away from them. They worried that having too much power in the hands of government would mean that, in time, they would be forced to fight for their freedom again. As a result, they were too cautious when they wrote the Articles of Confederation. The government was not able to levy the necessary taxes or create a strong enough military. The country was unable to keep order, for its central government lacked sufficient power and authority.

Drafting the Articles of Confederation

York Town, Pennsylvania 1777 13c USA

ARTICLES OF CONFEDERATION FIRST USA CONSTITUTION POSTAGE STAMP

GEORGE WASHINGTON

JAMES MADISON

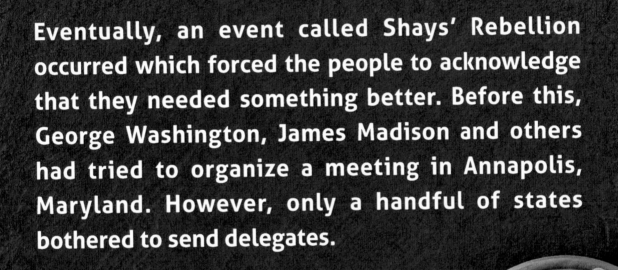

Eventually, an event called Shays' Rebellion occurred which forced the people to acknowledge that they needed something better. Before this, George Washington, James Madison and others had tried to organize a meeting in Annapolis, Maryland. However, only a handful of states bothered to send delegates.

However, now that Shay and his men had almost succeeded in robbing the federal weapons arsenal, it was realized that a new constitution would have to be made.

THE ENCOUNTER BETWEEN SHAYS'
REBELS AND GOVERNMENT TROOPS
BEFORE THE ARSENAL AT SPRINGFIELD,
MASSACHUSETTS ON 26 JANUARY 1787.

GEORGE WASHINGTON AT THE CONSTITUTIONAL CONVENTION WHICH TOOK PLACE FROM 25TH MAY TO 17TH SEPTEMBER 1787, IN PHILADELPHIA, PENNSYLVANIA.

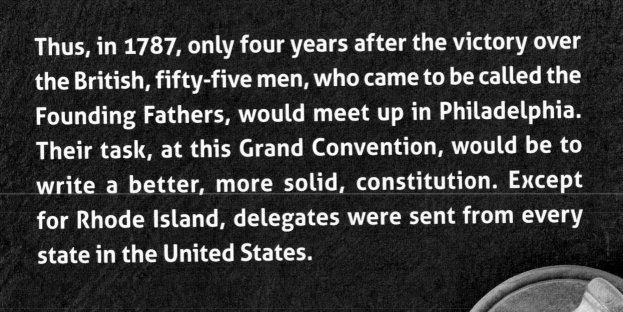

Thus, in 1787, only four years after the victory over the British, fifty-five men, who came to be called the Founding Fathers, would meet up in Philadelphia. Their task, at this Grand Convention, would be to write a better, more solid, constitution. Except for Rhode Island, delegates were sent from every state in the United States.

The convention was held in the State House which was the same place that in 1776 had birthed the Declaration of Independence. Today, it is called Independence Hall to honour its historical significance. The grand convention would begin on May 25 and end on September 17.

OLD STATE HOUSE LATER CALLED INDEPENDENCE HALL IN PHILADELPHIA

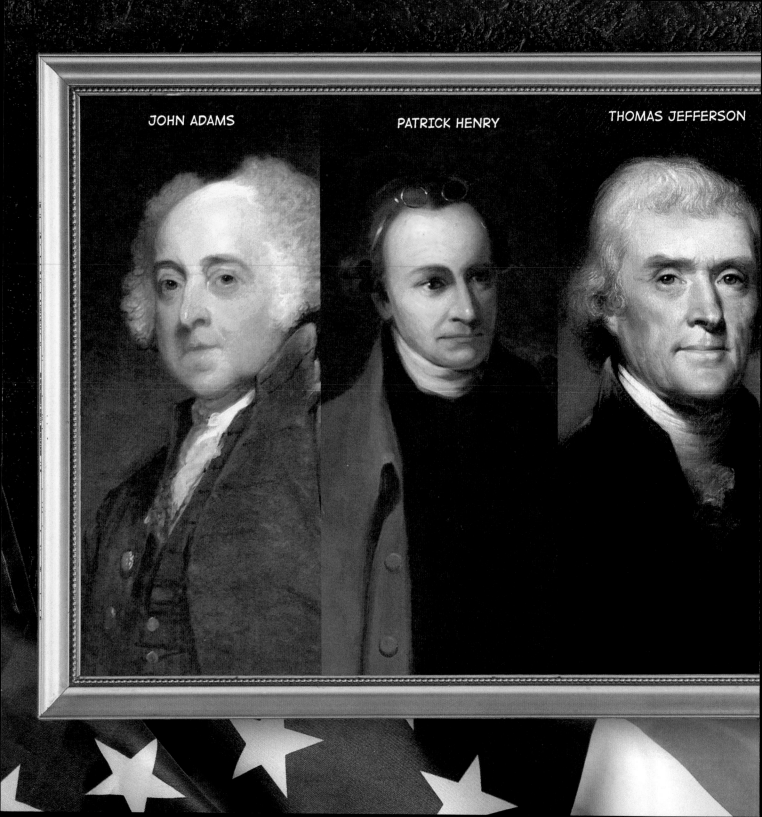

Some prominent people from the Revolutionary War, such as John Adams, Patrick Henry, and Thomas Jefferson did not attend this meeting. Patrick Henry was very skeptical and voiced concern about the meeting. He was afraid that this meeting would result in power being put in the wrong hands. He was not entirely wrong, however!

Although the meeting was originally held to find a way to improve the Articles of Confederation, the focus soon shifted to writing a new constitution. This constitution would replace the Articles of Confederation. Patrick Henry fought against the ratification as a result. He thought the delegates had taken things too far. Regardless, the constitution would pass and is now the oldest written constitution in the world.

SIGNING OF THE CONSTITUTION OF THE UNITED STATES ON SEPTEMBER 17, 1787.

THE FIRST PAGE OF
THE US CONSTITUTION

Although it was agreed that a new constitution should be written, the task of writing it would be far from easy. While at the constitutional convention, the delegates would have to discuss many different issues, and they did not always agree on what was the best thing to do. They knew that they needed a strong army, the ability to regulate trade, and a government that could levy taxes properly. However, they had to balance these objectives without taking too much power away from the people. A fair government would have to be created. Arguments would soon break out and compromises would have to be made.

A HOUSE DIVIDED

One of the biggest issues the Founding Fathers faced was that of equal representation in Congress. Congress was where different representatives from all the different states would meet to make new laws and abolish or amend old laws. The problem was that some states were much larger and had more people. These states thought they should have more representation as a result.

CONGRESS WAS WHERE DIFFERENT REPRESENTATIVES FROM ALL THE DIFFERENT STATES WOULD MEET TO MAKE NEW LAWS AND ABOLISH OR AMEND OLD LAWS.

VIRGINIA PLAN

Legislature
Bicameral

Representation
*Population based
(higher population yields more
representation)*

VISUAL REPRESENTATION OF THE STRUCTURE OF THE VIRGINIA PLAN.

One person cannot represent ten people as well as one person can represent five. For there to be equal opportunity for citizens to speak to their representative, and have their voices heard, larger states simply needed more people in congress. This was called the Virginia Plan and it was proposed by Edmund Randolph.

EDMUND RANDOLPH

The opposing idea was the New Jersey Plan which was proposed by William Paterson. He argued that the Virginia Plan was unfair. Every state had different interests and if the state with the most people were entitled to the most votes, they would always crush the rights and freedoms of the smaller states. He thought that every state should get the same number of votes. If the Virginia Plan were to be chosen, it would just mean that the larger states would rule over the smaller states! This concept can sometimes be called "tyranny of the majority".

NEW JERSEY PLAN

Legislature
Unicameral

Representation
State based
(each state equally represented)

VISUAL REPRESENTATION
OF THE STRUCTURE OF
THE NEW JERSEY PLAN.

CONSTITUTIONAL CONVENTION DEBATING THE FORM OF
THE NEW US GOVERNMENT AT PHILADELPHIA IN 1787.

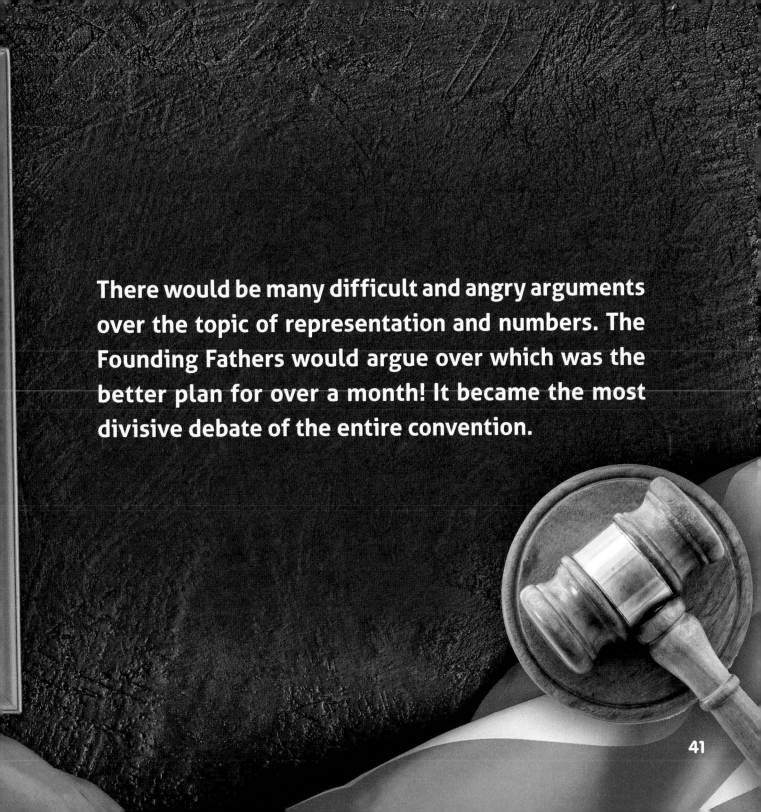

There would be many difficult and angry arguments over the topic of representation and numbers. The Founding Fathers would argue over which was the better plan for over a month! It became the most divisive debate of the entire convention.

The arguing became so tense that people from the smaller states even threatened to leave. If that had happened, the United States would have fallen apart. The discussion finally ended with what was called the Great Compromise. A compromise is when a disagreement is settled when both parties give something up to come to a place of agreement.

ROGER SHERMAN AND OLIVER ELLSWORTH IN 1787 DRAFTING THE GREAT (OR CONNECTICUT) COMPROMISE, A PLAN FOR REPRESENTATION IN CONGRESS.

SEAL OF THE U.S. HOUSE OF
REPRESENTATIVES

SEAL OF THE U.S. SENATE

The Great Compromise was suggested by Roger Sherman from Connecticut. It was accepted and the Founding Fathers decided that they would have two houses of Congress. One house would be called the House of Representatives and the other would be called the Senate.

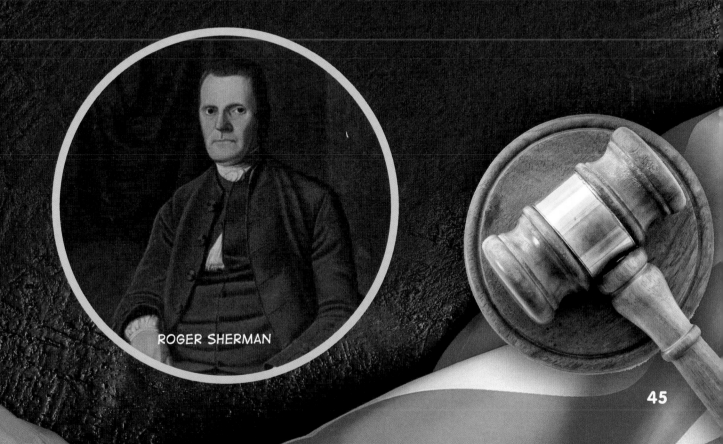

ROGER SHERMAN

The House of Representatives would have the number of representatives determined by how many people were in the various states. However, the number of representatives at the Senate would be equal, only two each. These members of Congress would be chosen through a general election in the various individual states. Both Houses would have to agree for a bill to become law.

THE GREAT COMPROMISE

Legislature
Bicameral

House of Representatives
each state is represented according to its population (satisfied the Virginia Plan)

Senate
each state has 2 senators (satisfied the New Jersey Plan)

Both houses of Congress must pass every law.

AN ILLUSTRATION OF THE STRUCTURE OF THE US SENATE AND HOUSE OF REPRESENTATIVES UNDER THE GREAT COMPROMISE.

THE POPULATION
OF SLAVES

There was another issue that became divisive during the Grand Convention. It was related to the issue of population, or the number of people in each state, and representation. The issue was whether slaves counted when determining population. If they counted, it would mean even more representatives to vote in the House of Representatives. If not, it would mean less voting power for states with slaves.

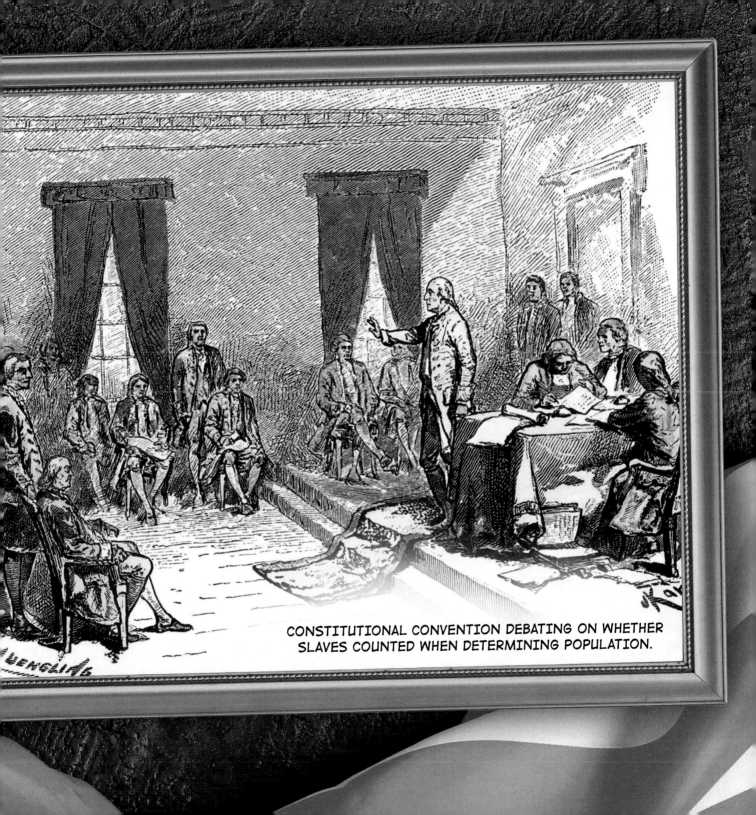

CONSTITUTIONAL CONVENTION DEBATING ON WHETHER SLAVES COUNTED WHEN DETERMINING POPULATION.

SLAVES GREETING A PLANTATION OWNER FAMILY IN THE SOUTH.

It was a very fraught issue. The whole point of having more representatives was to give the many people in each state an equal voice. If slaves were just property, they did not need a voice, but if they were people, they deserved representation. This led to a rigorous debate which was largely between the northern states and the southern states this time. Slavery was rampant in the South and the people there wanted their slaves counted so that they would be entitled to more votes, and with more votes, more political power.

However, the northerners, who were largely anti-slavery, thought the argument was absolutely absurd. Representatives were supposed to represent the interests and needs of the people. Slaves had no rights to anything under the southern law, so why should that mean the southern states get more representatives? It seemed like a clear ploy to give the southern states more power over the northerners.

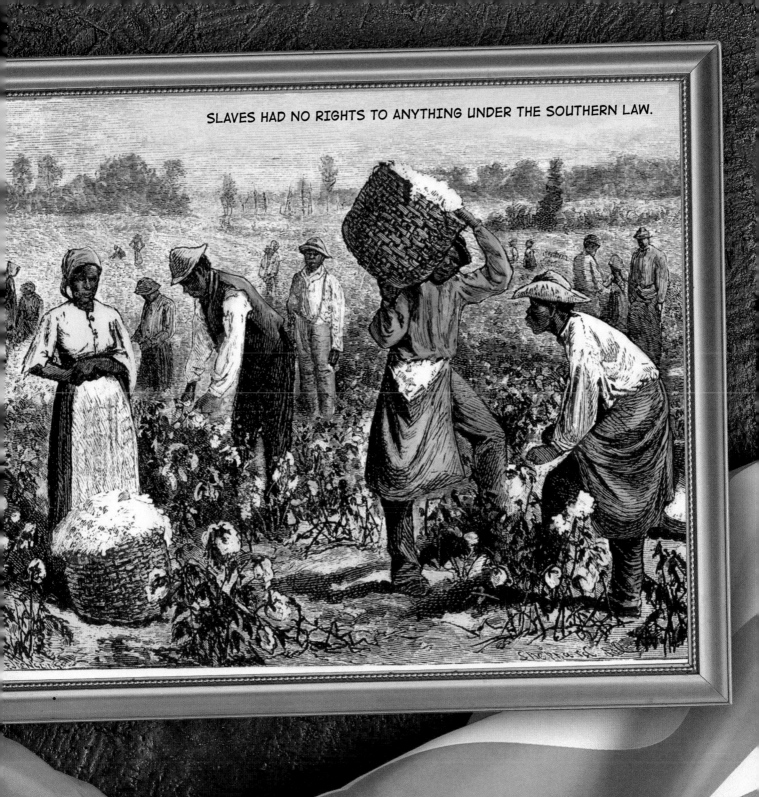

SLAVES HAD NO RIGHTS TO ANYTHING UNDER THE SOUTHERN LAW.

INSCRIPTION FROM THE
DECLARATION OF INDEPENDENCE
CARVED IN WHITE MARBLE ON
THE CURVED ROTUNDA WALL
OF THE THOMAS JEFFERSON
MEMORIAL IN WASHINGTON DC.

WE HOLD THESE TRUTHS TO BE SELF-EVIDENT: THAT ALL MEN ARE CREATED EQUAL, THAT THEY ARE ENDOWED BY THEIR CREATOR WITH CERTAIN INALIENABLE RIGHTS, AMONG THESE ARE LIFE, LIBERTY AND THE PURSUIT OF HAPPINESS, THAT TO SECURE THESE RIGHTS GOVERNMENTS ARE INSTITUTED AMONG MEN. WE··· SOLEMNLY PUBLISH AND DECLARE, THAT THESE COLONIES ARE AND OF RIGHT OUGHT TO BE FREE AND INDEPENDENT STATES···AND FOR THE SUPPORT OF THIS DECLARATION, WITH A FIRM RELIANCE ON THE PROTECTION OF DIVINE PROVIDENCE, WE MUTUALLY PLEDGE OUR LIVES, OUR FORTUNES AND OUR SACRED HONOUR.

More than that, the Declaration of Independence stated that "all men are created equal." It seemed to the northern states that to have slaves directly violated the intention of the Declaration. If slaves were men, and should be counted for the sake of representation, they deserved rights, freedoms, and equality same as everyone else. If the southerners wanted more votes, they needed to let the slaves vote! Otherwise, they were just seeking to make themselves too powerful at the expense of other people's freedoms!

THE DELEGATES OF THE CONVENTION
DECIDED TO TOLERATE SLAVERY.

Once again, the situation escalated so greatly that it looked as if the Grand Convention would fall apart and the United States would stop being united. South Carolina and Georgia refused to be a part of any country that would not allow slavery. Threatened by the thought of breaking up their new country, the delegates at the convention decided to tolerate slavery. Once again, there would be a compromise.

The compromises were "The Three-Fifths Compromise," "The Fugitive Slave Clause," and "The Slave Trade Compromise." The first compromise meant that for every five slaves, there would be three citizens counted. This meant that the South would get more votes, yet not as many as they had hoped.

THREE-FIFTHS COMPROMISE MEANT THAT FOR EVERY 5 SLAVES, THERE WOULD BE 3 CITIZENS COUNTED.

RUNAWAY SLAVES RETURNED TO
THEIR OWNERS DOWN SOUTH.

The next compromise meant that the constitution would require that if slaves escaped to the north, they would be returned to their owners down south. This was included since many northern abolitionists had been helping the slaves escape.

Finally, the last compromise meant that no new slaves would be allowed to be brought in from Africa after 1808, twenty years after the Grand Convention.

NO NEW SLAVES WOULD BE ALLOWED TO BE BROUGHT IN FROM AFRICA AFTER 1808.

GROUP OF SLAVES ESCAPING FOR THE NORTH

While these compromises were made, it did not solve the underlying issues. Were slaves entitled to rights? Should they vote? The people from the north were more inclined to help slaves gain freedom since the northern states were not primarily known for farming. However, down in the South, slaves were a significant part of the cotton and tobacco industries.

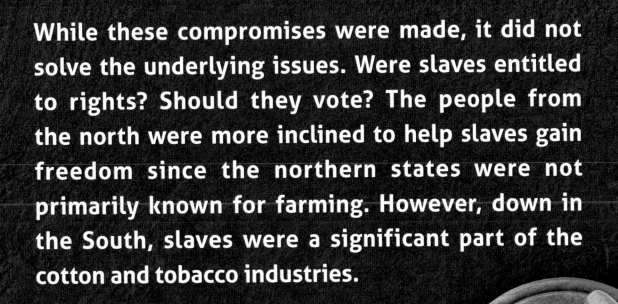

As a result, the southerners were not inclined to acknowledge the truth that slaves were human beings deserving of equality. It was how things has been there for generations and they did not want to change. However, eventually the issue would become so tense that it would lead to the American Civil War.

CONFEDERATE TROOPS ON THE MARCH
DURING THE AMERICAN CIVIL WAR.

After the Acts of Confederation proved to be ineffective, the colonists had to find a way to amend them. It soon became obvious that they would have to be replaced. A Grand Convention was held for this purpose where representatives from the colonies would meet. After many debates, compromises were made on several issues. The United States of America would have a constitution! To find out more information about the Grand Convention and the American Revolution, look for more Baby Professor books.

Visit

www.speedypublishing.com

To view and download free content on your favorite subject and browse our catalog of new and exciting books for readers of all ages.

Made in the USA
Monee, IL
18 November 2021

82475280R00045